MAXIMIZING
SUCCESS
JOURNAL

Sue Hawkes

INDEPENDENCE

Independence is loyalty to one's best self and principles and this is often disloyalty to the general idols and fetishes.

- Mark Twain

What does independence mean to me?

Where do I believe independence is most important?

Why?

Where do I believe independence is least important?

Why?

What causes me to act independently when collaboration may offer a more effective solution?

What causes me to act collaboratively when independence may offer a more effective solution?

When do I experience a need for independence?

When is independence a limitation?

When is independence most effective?

REFLECTING
ON THIS WEEK...

1. Describe the week that just ended in a few words:

2. Insights I have resulting from my experiences and observations of myself this week:

3. What were my greatest successes this week?

4. What new thoughts and behaviors am I aware of?

5. What am I most proud of?

6. What was surprising to me?

7. What am I most excited about?

8. Where do I need to dedicate more time?

9. What new actions/practices do I need to incorporate into my life?

10. What was most meaningful to me this week?

PREPARING
FOR THE COMING WEEK...

1 Looking ahead, what are my expectations for the coming week?

2 How will I be intentional with my time?

3 What's my focus for the week?

4 What do I need to prepare myself for?

5 What concerns do I have?

6 What am I most excited about?

7 What, if anything, needs to change this week?

8 Who do I need to connect with?

9 What or who do I need to say "no" to or let go of?

10 What would set me up to maximize success this week?

FREEDOM

We must be free not because we claim
freedom, but because we practice it.

- William Faulkner

What does freedom mean to me?

In what areas of my life do I experience the most freedom?

Why?

In what areas of my life do I experience the least freedom?

Why?

What influences whether I feel free or not?

How have I limited my choices?

When do I experience the most freedom?

Why is freedom important?

REFLECTING ON THIS WEEK...

1 Describe the week that just ended in a few words:

2 Insights I have resulting from my experiences and observations of myself this week:

3 What were my greatest successes this week?

4 What new thoughts and behaviors am I aware of?

5 What am I most proud of?

6 What was surprising to me?

7 What am I most excited about?

8 Where do I need to dedicate more time?

9 What new actions/practices do I need to incorporate into my life?

10 What was most meaningful to me this week?

PREPARING
FOR THE COMING WEEK...

1 Looking ahead, what are my expectations for the coming week?

2 How will I be intentional with my time?

3 What's my focus for the week?

4 What do I need to prepare myself for?

5 What concerns do I have?

6 What am I most excited about?

7 What, if anything, needs to change this week?

8 Who do I need to connect with?

9 What or who do I need to say "no" to or let go of?

10 What would set me up to maximize success this week?

INNOVATION

Innovation is the ability to see change as
an opportunity – not a threat.

- Steve Jobs

What does it mean to be innovative?

Where am I most innovative in my life?

THE ACT OF
INTRODUCING
SOMETHING
NEW

What innovations do I most appreciate?

Why?

In what ways can I be more innovative?

When is the last time I introduced something new into my life?

Why?

Who do I experience as an innovator?

■ What can I innovate today?

With whom?

REFLECTING
ON THIS WEEK...

1 Describe the week that just ended in a few words:

2 Insights I have resulting from my experiences and observations of myself this week:

3 What were my greatest successes this week?

4 What new thoughts and behaviors am I aware of?

5 What am I most proud of?

6 What was surprising to me?

7 What am I most excited about?

8 Where do I need to dedicate more time?

9 What new actions/practices do I need to incorporate into my life?

10 What was most meaningful to me this week?

PREPARING
FOR THE COMING WEEK...

1 Looking ahead, what are my expectations for the coming week?

2 How will I be intentional with my time?

3 What's my focus for the week?

4 What do I need to prepare myself for?

5 What concerns do I have?

6 What am I most excited about?

7 What, if anything, needs to change this week?

8 Who do I need to connect with?

9 What or who do I need to say "no" to or let go of?

10 What would set me up to maximize success this week?

DESIGN

Design is thinking made visible.

- Saul Bass

What does design mean to me?

How have I designed my life?

TO CONCEIVE OR FASHION IN THE MIND; INVENT

What areas of my life do I need to redesign?

What difference could that make?

When is design most important?

Who lives their life "by design?"

What do I notice about them?

When is the last time I sat down to design something?

What did I notice?

What does design make possible?

REFLECTING ON THIS WEEK...

1 Describe the week that just ended in a few words:

2 Insights I have resulting from my experiences and observations of myself this week:

3 What were my greatest successes this week?

4 What new thoughts and behaviors am I aware of?

5 What am I most proud of?

6 What was surprising to me?

7 What am I most excited about?

8 Where do I need to dedicate more time?

9 What new actions/practices do I need to incorporate into my life?

10 What was most meaningful to me this week?

PREPARING
FOR THE COMING WEEK...

1 Looking ahead, what are my expectations for the coming week?

2 How will I be intentional with my time?

3 What's my focus for the week?

4 What do I need to prepare myself for?

5 What concerns do I have?

6 What am I most excited about?

7 What, if anything, needs to change this week?

8 Who do I need to connect with?

9 What or who do I need to say "no" to or let go of?

10 What would set me up to maximize success this week?

TRANSFORMATION

Transformation is often more about
unlearning then learning.

- Richard Rohr

What does transformation mean to me?

Where am I transforming?

Where do I need to transform?

When is transformation easy for me?

When is it difficult?

What could benefit from transformation in my life?

How do I bring about change?

A MARKED
CHANGE

Where do I resist change?

What does transformation make possible?

REFLECTING ON THIS WEEK...

1 Describe the week that just ended in a few words:

2 Insights I have resulting from my experiences and observations of myself this week:

3 What were my greatest successes this week?

4 What new thoughts and behaviors am I aware of?

5 What am I most proud of?

6 What was surprising to me?

7 What am I most excited about?

8 Where do I need to dedicate more time?

9 What new actions/practices do I need to incorporate into my life?

10 What was most meaningful to me this week?

PREPARING
FOR THE COMING WEEK...

1 Looking ahead, what are my expectations for the coming week?

2 How will I be intentional with my time?

3 What's my focus for the week?

4 What do I need to prepare myself for?

5 What concerns do I have?

6 What am I most excited about?

7 What, if anything, needs to change this week?

8 Who do I need to connect with?

9 What or who do I need to say "no" to or let go of?

10 What would set me up to maximize success this week?

ABUNDANCE

Acknowledging the good that you already have in your life is the foundation for all abundance.

- Eckhart Tolle

What does abundance mean to me?

Where am I abundant in my life?

Who lives an abundant life?

What do I notice about them?

When I am abundant in my thinking, what is my experience of life?

What does abundance make possible?

FULLNESS TO
OVERFLOWING

How can I become more abundant?

Where can I become more abundant?

What could result?

REFLECTING ON THIS WEEK...

1 Describe the week that just ended in a few words:

2 Insights I have resulting from my experiences and observations of myself this week:

3 What were my greatest successes this week?

4 What new thoughts and behaviors am I aware of?

5 What am I most proud of?

6 What was surprising to me?

7 What am I most excited about?

8 Where do I need to dedicate more time?

9 What new actions/practices do I need to incorporate into my life?

10 What was most meaningful to me this week?

PREPARING
FOR THE COMING WEEK...

1 Looking ahead, what are my expectations for the coming week?

2 How will I be intentional with my time?

3 What's my focus for the week?

4 What do I need to prepare myself for?

5 What concerns do I have?

6 What am I most excited about?

7 What, if anything, needs to change this week?

8 Who do I need to connect with?

9 What or who do I need to say "no" to or let go of?

10 What would set me up to maximize success this week?

RELAXATION

Each person deserves a day away in which no problems are confronted, no solutions searched for. Each of us needs to withdraw from the cares which will not withdraw from us.

\- Maya Angelou

What does relaxation mean to me?

WEEK 33: RELAXATION
Refreshment of body or mind;
freedom from activity

How do I best relax?

WEEK 33: RELAXATION
Refreshment of body or mind;
freedom from activity

How could I relax more effectively?

REFRESHMENT
OF BODY
OR MIND;
FREEDOM
FROM
ACTIVITY

WEEK 33: RELAXATION
Refreshment of body or mind;
freedom from activity

When am I relaxed?

WEEK 33: RELAXATION
Refreshment of body or mind;
freedom from activity

What relaxation practices do I have?

What relaxation practices do I need?

WEEK 33: RELAXATION
Refreshment of body or mind;
freedom from activity

Why is relaxation important?

WEEK 33: RELAXATION
Refreshment of body or mind;
freedom from activity

Where am I most relaxed?

REFLECTING ON THIS WEEK...

1. Describe the week that just ended in a few words:

2. Insights I have resulting from my experiences and observations of myself this week:

3. What were my greatest successes this week?

4. What new thoughts and behaviors am I aware of?

5. What am I most proud of?

6. What was surprising to me?

7. What am I most excited about?

8. Where do I need to dedicate more time?

9. What new actions/practices do I need to incorporate into my life?

10. What was most meaningful to me this week?

PREPARING
FOR THE COMING WEEK...

1 Looking ahead, what are my expectations for the coming week?

2 How will I be intentional with my time?

3 What's my focus for the week?

4 What do I need to prepare myself for?

5 What concerns do I have?

6 What am I most excited about?

7 What, if anything, needs to change this week?

8 Who do I need to connect with?

9 What or who do I need to say "no" to or let go of?

10 What would set me up to maximize success this week?

RECREATION

People who cannot find time for recreation are
obliged sooner or later to find time for illness.

– John Wanamaker

WEEK 34: RECREATION
Refreshment of one's mind or body after work through
activity that amuses or stimulates; play

**What does recreation mean to me? In other words,
what does it mean to recreate?**

What do I do for recreation?

What is most refreshing for my mind or body?

REFRESHMENT OF ONE'S MIND OR BODY AFTER WORK THROUGH ACTIVITY THAT AMUSES OR STIMULATES; PLAY

Who do I enjoy playing with?

Why?

What recreation do I resist?

Why?

Why is recreation important?

How can I include more recreation in my life?

With whom?

REFLECTING
ON THIS WEEK...

1. Describe the week that just ended in a few words:

2. Insights I have resulting from my experiences and observations of myself this week:

3. What were my greatest successes this week?

4. What new thoughts and behaviors am I aware of?

5. What am I most proud of?

6. What was surprising to me?

7. What am I most excited about?

8. Where do I need to dedicate more time?

9. What new actions/practices do I need to incorporate into my life?

10. What was most meaningful to me this week?

PREPARING
FOR THE COMING WEEK...

1 Looking ahead, what are my expectations for the coming week?

2 How will I be intentional with my time?

3 What's my focus for the week?

4 What do I need to prepare myself for?

5 What concerns do I have?

6 What am I most excited about?

7 What, if anything, needs to change this week?

8 Who do I need to connect with?

9 What or who do I need to say "no" to or let go of?

10 What would set me up to maximize success this week?

JOY

A joyful life is not a floodlight of joy.
A joyful life is made up of joyful moments
gracefully strung together by trust, gratitude,
inspiration and faith.

- Brené Brown

It is not joy that makes us grateful, it is
gratitude that makes us joyful.

- Anonymous

What does joy mean to me?

When am I most joyful?

Who is joyful?

What do I notice about them?

INTENSE AND ESPECIALLY ECSTATIC OR EXULTANT HAPPINESS

When I'm joyful, how does it shape my experience?

With whom am I most joyful?

Why?

How can I bring joy to all I do today?

How can I bring joy consistently into my life?

REFLECTING
ON THIS WEEK...

1 Describe the week that just ended in a few words:

2 Insights I have resulting from my experiences and observations of myself this week:

3 What were my greatest successes this week?

4 What new thoughts and behaviors am I aware of?

5 What am I most proud of?

6 What was surprising to me?

7 What am I most excited about?

8 Where do I need to dedicate more time?

9 What new actions/practices do I need to incorporate into my life?

10 What was most meaningful to me this week?

PREPARING
FOR THE COMING WEEK...

1   Looking ahead, what are my expectations for the coming week?

2   How will I be intentional with my time?

3   What's my focus for the week?

4   What do I need to prepare myself for?

5   What concerns do I have?

6   What am I most excited about?

7   What, if anything, needs to change this week?

8   Who do I need to connect with?

9   What or who do I need to say "no" to or let go of?

10   What would set me up to maximize success this week?

CONNECTEDNESS

I do believe in an everyday sort of magic — the inexplicable connectedness we sometimes experience with places, people, works of art and the like; the eerie appropriateness of moments of synchronicity; the whispered voice, the hidden presence, when we think we're alone.

- Charles de Lint

What does it mean to be connected?

When do I experience my greatest sense of connectedness?

What connections do I notice most in my life?

Who am I most connected to?

How do I know?

How can i connect with people fully today?

A RELATION
BETWEEN
THINGS OR
EVENTS

What is my experience when I feel disconnected?

When do I notice it occurring?

CONNEC

How can I consistently appreciate the connections in life?

EDNESS

REFLECTING ON THIS WEEK...

1 Describe the week that just ended in a few words:

2 Insights I have resulting from my experiences and observations of myself this week:

3 What were my greatest successes this week?

4 What new thoughts and behaviors am I aware of?

5 What am I most proud of?

6 What was surprising to me?

7 What am I most excited about?

8 Where do I need to dedicate more time?

9 What new actions/practices do I need to incorporate into my life?

10 What was most meaningful to me this week?

PREPARING
FOR THE COMING WEEK...

1 Looking ahead, what are my expectations for the coming week?

2 How will I be intentional with my time?

3 What's my focus for the week?

4 What do I need to prepare myself for?

5 What concerns do I have?

6 What am I most excited about?

7 What, if anything, needs to change this week?

8 Who do I need to connect with?

9 What or who do I need to say "no" to or let go of?

10 What would set me up to maximize success this week?

INTIMACY

Intimacy is being seen and known as the person you truly are.

- Amy Bloom

Intimacy = Into me see.

- Author Unknown

What does intimacy mean to me?

One definition of intimacy is "into me see." How open am I to others being intimate with me?

With whom am I most intimate?

What contributes to your relationship being intimate?

When am I most intimate?

Why?

How can I deepen my intimacy with others?

What do I notice when I intimately engage with someone?

How can I allow more intimacy in my life?

RELATING TO
OR INDICATIVE
OF ONE'S
DEEPEST
NATURE;
ESSENTIAL,
INNERMOST

REFLECTING
ON THIS WEEK...

1 Describe the week that just ended in a few words:

2 Insights I have resulting from my experiences and observations of myself this week:

3 What were my greatest successes this week?

4 What new thoughts and behaviors am I aware of?

5 What am I most proud of?

6 What was surprising to me?

7 What am I most excited about?

8 Where do I need to dedicate more time?

9 What new actions/practices do I need to incorporate into my life?

10 What was most meaningful to me this week?

PREPARING
FOR THE COMING WEEK...

1 Looking ahead, what are my expectations for the coming week?

2 How will I be intentional with my time?

3 What's my focus for the week?

4 What do I need to prepare myself for?

5 What concerns do I have?

6 What am I most excited about?

7 What, if anything, needs to change this week?

8 Who do I need to connect with?

9 What or who do I need to say "no" to or let go of?

10 What would set me up to maximize success this week?

COMPASSION

Until you have real compassion,
you cannot recognize love.

- Bob Thurman

WEEK 38: COMPASSION
A deep awareness of and sympathy
for another's suffering

What does compassion mean to me?

When am I most compassionate?

When am I least compassionate?

WEEK 38: COMPASSION
A deep awareness of and sympathy
for another's suffering

What is my experience of people being compassionate with me?

WEEK 38: COMPASSION
A deep awareness of and sympathy
for another's suffering

What is my experience of being compassionate with others?

A DEEP
AWARENESS OF
AND SYMPATHY
FOR ANOTHER'S
SUFFERING

Where could I be more compassionate?

WEEK 38: COMPASSION
A deep awareness of and sympathy
for another's suffering

How can I express compassion today?

REFLECTING
ON THIS WEEK...

1. Describe the week that just ended in a few words:

2. Insights I have resulting from my experiences and observations of myself this week:

3. What were my greatest successes this week?

4. What new thoughts and behaviors am I aware of?

5. What am I most proud of?

6. What was surprising to me?

7. What am I most excited about?

8. Where do I need to dedicate more time?

9. What new actions/practices do I need to incorporate into my life?

10. What was most meaningful to me this week?

PREPARING
FOR THE COMING WEEK...

1 Looking ahead, what are my expectations for the coming week?

2 How will I be intentional with my time?

3 What's my focus for the week?

4 What do I need to prepare myself for?

5 What concerns do I have?

6 What am I most excited about?

7 What, if anything, needs to change this week?

8 Who do I need to connect with?

9 What or who do I need to say "no" to or let go of?

10 What would set me up to maximize success this week?

FORGIVENESS

Forgiveness is not about letting someone
off the hook for their actions,
but freeing ourselves of negative
energies that bind us to them.

- Satsuki Shibuya

Forgiveness is giving up the hope
that the past could have been any different.

- Oprah Winfrey

What does forgiveness mean to me?

What's the forgiveness I've been unwilling to offer?

When is it easy for me to forgive?

When is it difficult for me to forgive?

Who do I need to forgive?

TO RENOUNCE
ANGER OR
RESENTMENT
AGAINST

How can I be more forgiving?

What experience does forgiveness offer?

REFLECTING
ON THIS WEEK...

1 Describe the week that just ended in a few words:

2 Insights I have resulting from my experiences and observations of myself this week:

3 What were my greatest successes this week?

4 What new thoughts and behaviors am I aware of?

5 What am I most proud of?

6 What was surprising to me?

7 What am I most excited about?

8 Where do I need to dedicate more time?

9 What new actions/practices do I need to incorporate into my life?

10 What was most meaningful to me this week?

PREPARING
FOR THE COMING WEEK...

1. Looking ahead, what are my expectations for the coming week?

2. How will I be intentional with my time?

3. What's my focus for the week?

4. What do I need to prepare myself for?

5. What concerns do I have?

6. What am I most excited about?

7. What, if anything, needs to change this week?

8. Who do I need to connect with?

9. What or who do I need to say "no" to or let go of?

10. What would set me up to maximize success this week?

LISTENING

The most basic and powerful way to connect
to another person is to listen. Just listen.
Perhaps the most important thing we ever give
each other is our attention. A loving silence
often has far more power to heal and to
connect than the most well-intentioned words.

- Rachel Naomi Remen

What does listening mean in my life?

What do I notice when I'm being fully listened to?

What do I notice when I'm fully listening to another person?

THE ACT
OF HEARING
ATTENTIVELY

How often do I fully listen?

When do I fully listen to others?

Who listens fully to me?

How can I be fully present and listen to others consistently?

REFLECTING
ON THIS WEEK...

1 Describe the week that just ended in a few words:

2 Insights I have resulting from my experiences and observations of myself this week:

3 What were my greatest successes this week?

4 What new thoughts and behaviors am I aware of?

5 What am I most proud of?

6 What was surprising to me?

7 What am I most excited about?

8 Where do I need to dedicate more time?

9 What new actions/practices do I need to incorporate into my life?

10 What was most meaningful to me this week?

PREPARING
FOR THE COMING WEEK...

1 Looking ahead, what are my expectations for the coming week?

2 How will I be intentional with my time?

3 What's my focus for the week?

4 What do I need to prepare myself for?

5 What concerns do I have?

6 What am I most excited about?

7 What, if anything, needs to change this week?

8 Who do I need to connect with?

9 What or who do I need to say "no" to or let go of?

10 What would set me up to maximize success this week?

SERENITY

My soul yearns for stillness, for a space, serenity; where I can be silent and by doing so I come to a deeper sense of myself and my place in the universe. Silence is not an absence but a presence, not an emptiness but a filling up.

- Yvonne

What does serenity mean to me?

How often do I experience serenity?

Where do I experience serenity?

What contributes most to my serenity?

When am I most serene?

THE ABSENCE OF
MENTAL STRESS
OR ANXIETY

How can I increase my serenity?

What can I do to contribute to other people's serenity?

REFLECTING
ON THIS WEEK...

1 Describe the week that just ended in a few words:

2 Insights I have resulting from my experiences and observations of myself this week:

3 What were my greatest successes this week?

4 What new thoughts and behaviors am I aware of?

5 What am I most proud of?

6 What was surprising to me?

7 What am I most excited about?

8 Where do I need to dedicate more time?

9 What new actions/practices do I need to incorporate into my life?

10 What was most meaningful to me this week?

PREPARING
FOR THE COMING WEEK...

1. Looking ahead, what are my expectations for the coming week?

2. How will I be intentional with my time?

3. What's my focus for the week?

4. What do I need to prepare myself for?

5. What concerns do I have?

6. What am I most excited about?

7. What, if anything, needs to change this week?

8. Who do I need to connect with?

9. What or who do I need to say "no" to or let go of?

10. What would set me up to maximize success this week?

INSPIRATION

Don't waste time waiting for inspiration;
begin, and inspiration will find you.

- H. Jackson Brown, Jr.

WEEK 42: INSPIRATION
The process of being mentally stimulated to do or feel
something, especially to do something meaningful.

What does inspiration mean to me?

Where do I draw my inspiration from?

What am I inspired by?

WEEK 42: INSPIRATION

The process of being mentally stimulated to do or feel
something, especially to do something meaningful.

Who am I inspired by?

When am I most inspired?

What's my experience when I'm inspired?

INSPII

WEEK 42: INSPIRATION
The process of being mentally stimulated to do or feel
something, especially to do something meaningful.

How can I be an inspiration to others today?

RATION

REFLECTING
ON THIS WEEK...

1 Describe the week that just ended in a few words:

2 Insights I have resulting from my experiences and observations of myself this week:

3 What were my greatest successes this week?

4 What new thoughts and behaviors am I aware of?

5 What am I most proud of?

6 What was surprising to me?

7 What am I most excited about?

8 Where do I need to dedicate more time?

9 What new actions/practices do I need to incorporate into my life?

10 What was most meaningful to me this week?

PREPARING
FOR THE COMING WEEK...

1 Looking ahead, what are my expectations for the coming week?

2 How will I be intentional with my time?

3 What's my focus for the week?

4 What do I need to prepare myself for?

5 What concerns do I have?

6 What am I most excited about?

7 What, if anything, needs to change this week?

8 Who do I need to connect with?

9 What or who do I need to say "no" to or let go of?

10 What would set me up to maximize success this week?

PARTNERSHIP

Partnership is two unique people who bring out
the very best in each other and who know that
even though they are wonderful as individuals,
they are even better together.

- Author Unknown

What does partnership mean to me?

WEEK 43: PARTNERSHIP
A relationship between individuals or groups that is
characterized by mutual cooperation and responsibility

Who do I have an extraordinary partnership with?

How could I be a better partner?

What is my experience of partnership?

How do I limit my partnerships?

A RELATIONSHIP BETWEEN INDIVIDUALS OR GROUPS THAT IS CHARACTERIZED BY MUTUAL COOPERATION AND RESPONSIBILITY

Where could I expand my partnerships?

WEEK 43: PARTNERSHIP
A relationship between individuals or groups that is
characterized by mutual cooperation and responsibility

How can I be a better partner to others?

REFLECTING
ON THIS WEEK...

1 Describe the week that just ended in a few words:

2 Insights I have resulting from my experiences and observations of myself this week:

3 What were my greatest successes this week?

4 What new thoughts and behaviors am I aware of?

5 What am I most proud of?

6 What was surprising to me?

7 What am I most excited about?

8 Where do I need to dedicate more time?

9 What new actions/practices do I need to incorporate into my life?

10 What was most meaningful to me this week?

PREPARING
FOR THE COMING WEEK...

1 Looking ahead, what are my expectations for the coming week?

2 How will I be intentional with my time?

3 What's my focus for the week?

4 What do I need to prepare myself for?

5 What concerns do I have?

6 What am I most excited about?

7 What, if anything, needs to change this week?

8 Who do I need to connect with?

9 What or who do I need to say "no" to or let go of?

10 What would set me up to maximize success this week?

SERVICE

Service to others is the rent you pay for
your room here on earth.

- Muhammad Ali

The best way to find yourself is to lose
yourself in the service of others.

- Mahatma Gandhi

What does service mean to me?

Where is service important in my life?

Who do I experience as a servant leader?

What do I notice about them?

Where could I serve more effectively?

Who is in service to me?

AN ACT OF
ASSISTANCE
OR BENEFIT

How could I serve today?

What is my experience when someone is in service to me?

REFLECTING ON THIS WEEK...

1 Describe the week that just ended in a few words:

2 Insights I have resulting from my experiences and observations of myself this week:

3 What were my greatest successes this week?

4 What new thoughts and behaviors am I aware of?

5 What am I most proud of?

6 What was surprising to me?

7 What am I most excited about?

8 Where do I need to dedicate more time?

9 What new actions/practices do I need to incorporate into my life?

10 What was most meaningful to me this week?

PREPARING
FOR THE COMING WEEK...

1 Looking ahead, what are my expectations for the coming week?

2 How will I be intentional with my time?

3 What's my focus for the week?

4 What do I need to prepare myself for?

5 What concerns do I have?

6 What am I most excited about?

7 What, if anything, needs to change this week?

8 Who do I need to connect with?

9 What or who do I need to say "no" to or let go of?

10 What would set me up to maximize success this week?

BEAUTY

Everything has beauty,
but not everyone sees it.

- Confucius

WEEK 45: BEAUTY
The quality that gives pleasure to the mind or senses
and is associated with such properties as harmony of form or
color, excellence of artistry, truthfulness, and originality.

What do I experience as beautiful?

WEEK 45: BEAUTY
The quality that gives pleasure to the mind or senses
and is associated with such properties as harmony of form or
color, excellence of artistry, truthfulness, and originality.

Where is harmony most present in my life?

WEEK 45: BEAUTY
The quality that gives pleasure to the mind or senses
and is associated with such properties as harmony of form or
color, excellence of artistry, truthfulness, and originality.

How does beauty show up in my life?

WEEK 45: BEAUTY
The quality that gives pleasure to the mind or senses
and is associated with such properties as harmony of form or
color, excellence of artistry, truthfulness, and originality.

What gives pleasure to my mind and senses?

What and who do I recognize as beautiful?

THE QUALITY THAT GIVES PLEASURE TO THE MIND OR SENSES AND IS ASSOCIATED WITH SUCH PROPERTIES AS HARMONY OF FORM OR COLOR, EXCELLENCE OF ARTISTRY, TRUTHFULNESS, AND ORIGINALITY.

WEEK 45: BEAUTY
The quality that gives pleasure to the mind or senses
and is associated with such properties as harmony of form or
color, excellence of artistry, truthfulness, and originality.

What can I do to enhance the beauty I experience today?

How can I recognize beauty in my life consistently?

REFLECTING ON THIS WEEK...

1. Describe the week that just ended in a few words:

2. Insights I have resulting from my experiences and observations of myself this week:

3. What were my greatest successes this week?

4. What new thoughts and behaviors am I aware of?

5. What am I most proud of?

6. What was surprising to me?

7. What am I most excited about?

8. Where do I need to dedicate more time?

9. What new actions/practices do I need to incorporate into my life?

10. What was most meaningful to me this week?

PREPARING
FOR THE COMING WEEK...

1 Looking ahead, what are my expectations for the coming week?

2 How will I be intentional with my time?

3 What's my focus for the week?

4 What do I need to prepare myself for?

5 What concerns do I have?

6 What am I most excited about?

7 What, if anything, needs to change this week?

8 Who do I need to connect with?

9 What or who do I need to say "no" to or let go of?

10 What would set me up to maximize success this week?

KINDNESS

Unexpected kindness is the most powerful,
least costly, and most underrated agent
of human change.

- Bob Kerrey

What does kindness mean to me?

WEEK 46: KINDNESS
The quality of being warm-hearted,
humane and sympathetic

What is my experience of people being kind to me?

WEEK 46: KINDNESS
The quality of being warm-hearted,
humane and sympathetic

What is my experience while being kind to others?

THE QUALITY
OF BEING
WARM-HEARTED,
HUMANE AND
SYMPATHETIC

WEEK 46: KINDNESS
The quality of being warm-hearted,
humane and sympathetic

How can I express kindness today?

How can I appreciate and experience kindness fully?

Who is kind to me?

What is my experience?

Where can I bring more kindness into my life?

REFLECTING ON THIS WEEK...

1 Describe the week that just ended in a few words:

2 Insights I have resulting from my experiences and observations of myself this week:

3 What were my greatest successes this week?

4 What new thoughts and behaviors am I aware of?

5 What am I most proud of?

6 What was surprising to me?

7 What am I most excited about?

8 Where do I need to dedicate more time?

9 What new actions/practices do I need to incorporate into my life?

10 What was most meaningful to me this week?

PREPARING
FOR THE COMING WEEK...

1 Looking ahead, what are my expectations for the coming week?

2 How will I be intentional with my time?

3 What's my focus for the week?

4 What do I need to prepare myself for?

5 What concerns do I have?

6 What am I most excited about?

7 What, if anything, needs to change this week?

8 Who do I need to connect with?

9 What or who do I need to say "no" to or let go of?

10 What would set me up to maximize success this week?

CONSIDERATION

If we were to make the conscious and frequent effort of treating others with consideration, the effects on us and on society as a whole would be amazing.

- Henry Charles Link

What does it mean to be considerate?

Who is most considerate in my life?

Where am I considerate in my life?

When is consideration most important to me?

How can I be considerate today?

KIND REGARD
FOR OTHERS

What consideration can I bring to others today?

Where can I be more considerate?

REFLECTING
ON THIS WEEK...

1. Describe the week that just ended in a few words:

2. Insights I have resulting from my experiences and observations of myself this week:

3. What were my greatest successes this week?

4. What new thoughts and behaviors am I aware of?

5. What am I most proud of?

6. What was surprising to me?

7. What am I most excited about?

8. Where do I need to dedicate more time?

9. What new actions/practices do I need to incorporate into my life?

10. What was most meaningful to me this week?

PREPARING
FOR THE COMING WEEK...

1. Looking ahead, what are my expectations for the coming week?

2. How will I be intentional with my time?

3. What's my focus for the week?

4. What do I need to prepare myself for?

5. What concerns do I have?

6. What am I most excited about?

7. What, if anything, needs to change this week?

8. Who do I need to connect with?

9. What or who do I need to say "no" to or let go of?

10. What would set me up to maximize success this week?

GENEROSITY

No one has ever become poor by giving.

- Anne Frank

Generosity is the most
natural outward expression of an inner
attitude of compassion.

- Author Unknown

What does generosity mean to me?

Who do I experience as generous?

What do I notice?

Where is generosity most present for me?

How can I be generous today?

Where can I be more generous?

LIBERALITY
IN GIVING OR
WILLINGNESS
TO GIVE

What do I experience when someone is generous with m

How can I express generosity fully?

REFLECTING
ON THIS WEEK...

1 Describe the week that just ended in a few words:

2 Insights I have resulting from my experiences and observations of myself this week:

3 What were my greatest successes this week?

4 What new thoughts and behaviors am I aware of?

5 What am I most proud of?

6 What was surprising to me?

7 What am I most excited about?

8 Where do I need to dedicate more time?

9 What new actions/practices do I need to incorporate into my life?

10 What was most meaningful to me this week?

PREPARING
FOR THE COMING WEEK...

1 Looking ahead, what are my expectations for the coming week?

2 How will I be intentional with my time?

3 What's my focus for the week?

4 What do I need to prepare myself for?

5 What concerns do I have?

6 What am I most excited about?

7 What, if anything, needs to change this week?

8 Who do I need to connect with?

9 What or who do I need to say "no" to or let go of?

10 What would set me up to maximize success this week?

WEEK 49

ACKNOWLEDGEMENT

The acknowledgement of a single
possibility can change everything.

- Aberjhani

What does acknowledgment mean to me?

Who do I need to acknowledge?

Who acknowledges me?

What is my experience?

AN EXPRESSION OF THANKS OR A TOKEN OF APPRECIATION

How do I most like to be acknowledged?

Where could I acknowledge people more fully?

What do I want to most acknowledge myself for?

How can I authentically acknowledge people today?

REFLECTING
ON THIS WEEK...

1 Describe the week that just ended in a few words:

2 Insights I have resulting from my experiences and observations of myself this week:

3 What were my greatest successes this week?

4 What new thoughts and behaviors am I aware of?

5 What am I most proud of?

6 What was surprising to me?

7 What am I most excited about?

8 Where do I need to dedicate more time?

9 What new actions/practices do I need to incorporate into my life?

10 What was most meaningful to me this week?

PREPARING
FOR THE COMING WEEK...

1 Looking ahead, what are my expectations for the coming week?

2 How will I be intentional with my time?

3 What's my focus for the week?

4 What do I need to prepare myself for?

5 What concerns do I have?

6 What am I most excited about?

7 What, if anything, needs to change this week?

8 Who do I need to connect with?

9 What or who do I need to say "no" to or let go of?

10 What would set me up to maximize success this week?

APPRECIATION

Appreciation can make a day, even change a life. Your willingness to put it into words is all that is necessary.

- Margaret Cousins

WEEK 50: APPRECIATION
Recognition of the quality, value, significance,
or magnitude of people and things

What does appreciation mean to me?

WEEK 50: APPRECIATION
Recognition of the quality, value, significance,
or magnitude of people and things

Who do I appreciate in my life?

WEEK 50: APPRECIATION
Recognition of the quality, value, significance,
or magnitude of people and things

Where do I experience appreciation fully?

RECOGNITION
OF THE
QUALITY, VALUE,
SIGNIFICANCE,
OR MAGNITUDE
OF PEOPLE
AND THINGS

Who could I appreciate more fully?

How can I better appreciate myself?

Others?

WEEK 50: APPRECIATION
Recognition of the quality, value, significance,
or magnitude of people and things

What do I most appreciate about my life?

How can I create and experience appreciation today?

REFLECTING ON THIS WEEK...

1 Describe the week that just ended in a few words:

2 Insights I have resulting from my experiences and observations of myself this week:

3 What were my greatest successes this week?

4 What new thoughts and behaviors am I aware of?

5 What am I most proud of?

6 What was surprising to me?

7 What am I most excited about?

8 Where do I need to dedicate more time?

9 What new actions/practices do I need to incorporate into my life?

10 What was most meaningful to me this week?

PREPARING
FOR THE COMING WEEK...

1 Looking ahead, what are my expectations for the coming week?

2 How will I be intentional with my time?

3 What's my focus for the week?

4 What do I need to prepare myself for?

5 What concerns do I have?

6 What am I most excited about?

7 What, if anything, needs to change this week?

8 Who do I need to connect with?

9 What or who do I need to say "no" to or let go of?

10 What would set me up to maximize success this week?

GRATITUDE

You simply will not be the same person
two months from now after consciously giving
thanks each day for the abundance that exists
in your life. And you will have set in motion an
ancient spiritual law: The more you have and
are grateful for, the more will be given to you.

- Sarah Ban Breathnach

What does gratitude mean to me?

What am I most grateful for in my life?

How does gratitude reveal itself in my life?

What's my experience when I'm being grateful?

What's my experience being thankful for others?

THANKFULNESS

Who am I most grateful for?

How can I express and experience gratitude today?

REFLECTING ON THIS WEEK...

1 Describe the week that just ended in a few words:

2 Insights I have resulting from my experiences and observations of myself this week:

3 What were my greatest successes this week?

4 What new thoughts and behaviors am I aware of?

5 What am I most proud of?

6 What was surprising to me?

7 What am I most excited about?

8 Where do I need to dedicate more time?

9 What new actions/practices do I need to incorporate into my life?

10 What was most meaningful to me this week?

PREPARING
FOR THE COMING WEEK...

1 Looking ahead, what are my expectations for the coming week?

2 How will I be intentional with my time?

3 What's my focus for the week?

4 What do I need to prepare myself for?

5 What concerns do I have?

6 What am I most excited about?

7 What, if anything, needs to change this week?

8 Who do I need to connect with?

9 What or who do I need to say "no" to or let go of?

10 What would set me up to maximize success this week?

GRACE

Grace has been defined as the outward
expression of the inward harmony of the soul.

- William Hazlitt

What does grace mean to me?

How is grace present in my life?

When do I experience grace?

Who do I experience grace from?

Who do I offer grace to?

THE FREE AND UNMERITED FAVOR OR BENEFICENCE OF GOD

What contributes most to my expression of grace?

How can I express and experience grace today?

REFLECTING ON THIS WEEK...

1. Describe the week that just ended in a few words:

2. Insights I have resulting from my experiences and observations of myself this week:

3. What were my greatest successes this week?

4. What new thoughts and behaviors am I aware of?

5. What am I most proud of?

6. What was surprising to me?

7. What am I most excited about?

8. Where do I need to dedicate more time?

9. What new actions/practices do I need to incorporate into my life?

10. What was most meaningful to me this week?

PREPARING
FOR THE COMING WEEK...

1 Looking ahead, what are my expectations for the coming week?

2 How will I be intentional with my time?

3 What's my focus for the week?

4 What do I need to prepare myself for?

5 What concerns do I have?

6 What am I most excited about?

7 What, if anything, needs to change this week?

8 Who do I need to connect with?

9 What or who do I need to say "no" to or let go of?

10 What would set me up to maximize success this week?

INTEGRITY

Live in such a way that if someone spoke badly
of you no one would believe it.

- Author Unknown

One of the truest tests of integrity
is its blunt refusal to be compromised.

- Chinua Achebe

WEEK 53: INTEGRITY
The quality or condition of being whole
or undivided; completeness

What does integrity mean to me?

WEEK 53: INTEGRITY
The quality or condition of being whole
or undivided; completeness

What am I most proud to have completed this year?

What do I need to complete to begin the new year with integrity?

THE QUALITY OR CONDITION OF BEING WHOLE OR UNDIVIDED; COMPLETENESS

REFLECTING
ON YOUR LAST
WEEK...

1 Describe the week that just ended in a few words:

2 Insights I have resulting from my experiences and observations of myself this week:

3 What were my greatest successes this week?

4 What new thoughts and behaviors am I aware of?

5 What am I most proud of?

6 What was surprising to me?

7 What am I most excited about?

8 Where do I need to dedicate more time?

9 What new actions/practices do I need to incorporate into my life?

10 What was most meaningful to me this week?

The reality remains that being a leader requires taking risks, creating opportunities out of problems, and venturing out onto the skinny branches. That's where you, as a leader, are at your best, and it isn't easy. Venturing onto those branches is accompanied by your humanity, which includes vulnerability. As Patrick Lencioni says, "*Success is not a matter of mastering subtle, sophisticated theory, but rather of embracing common sense with uncommon levels of discipline and persistence.*"

In order to maximize success, you must have practices to shatter the illusions you have and stop chasing perfection. The questions contained in this journal are introspective, offering you the opportunity to gain perspective about yourself as a leader. By answering them, you will begin to reach a place where you're truly at peace and in touch with yourself, and nothing anyone says or does bothers you, and no negativity or drama can touch you. You'll reach the pinnacle of whatever you do; as the ultimate leader you can be. This IS it; you're at the top of your game, the desired space to be; you're Unf♥<kwithable.

To see where you land on the Unf♥<kwithability scale, visit our website at: www.ChasingPerfection.net/unfscale

STAY CONNECTED & JOIN THE MOVEMENT

Check out the book, audiobook and workbook.

EMAIL:
info@sayyess.com

WEBSITES:
www.sayyess.com
www.suehawkes.com
www.ChasingPerfection.net

BLOG:
www.ChasingPerfection.net/blog

FACEBOOK:
www.facebook.com/ChasingPerfectionBook

TWITTER:
@SueHawkesYESS

LINKEDIN:
www.linkedin.com/in/suehawkes

INSTAGRAM:
@suehawkes

OFFICE PHONE:
612-718-1699